Goodbye
Dublin

BELFAST

IRISH SEA

Manchester

erpool

Manchester
Airport

DUBLIN

Chester

Liz Lewis

CARDIFF

**Geographical
Association**

It is raining when Barnaby goes to the airport. He can not see out for the rain on the bus windows.

Barnaby checks in at the airport.

The plane is ready to go at seven o'clock.

'Good evening, everyone. Have a good flight.' says the pilot.

As the plane gets higher and higher the
houses look smaller and smaller.

Photo: Jefferson Air Photography

5

Suddenly Barnaby can only see grey cloud. The plane is flying through a rain cloud.

How will we find our way home?

Don't worry Barnaby, the pilot has a compass to help find the way. Would you like to see?

Laura, the flight attendant, takes
Barnaby to see the pilot.

As the plane flies
out of the cloud
Barnaby can
see a beautiful
sunset. The
clouds are
gold and
pink.

Barnaby counts all the different colours he can see.

'We will land
in ten minutes,'
says the pilot.
'You can see
the lights of
England if
you look out.'

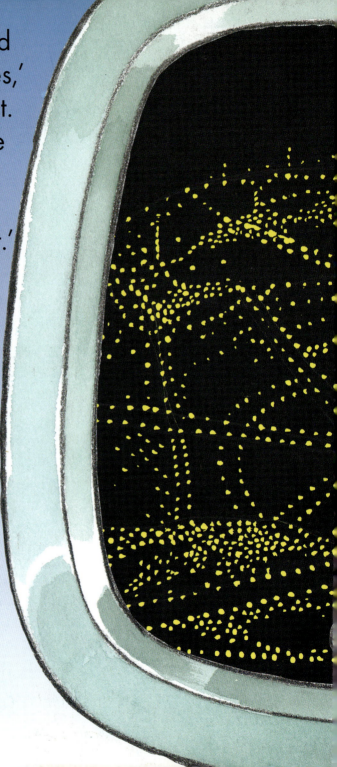

Barnaby can see groups of lights where there are towns, and long lines where there are roads.